PRESSURE COOKING!

USING A LITTLE PRESSURE TO CREATE EASY & DELICIOUS MEALS!

Connie Neckels

Pascoe Publishing, Inc.
Rocklin, CA

Cover and Page Design by Kayla Blanco
Production Coordination by Debi Bock

ISBN: 978-1-929862-70-2

08   09   10

10   9   8   7   6   5   4   3

Published in the United States of America by

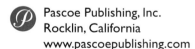

Pascoe Publishing, Inc.
Rocklin, California
www.pascoepublishing.com

Printed in the United States of America

TABLE OF CONTENTS

INTRODUCTION

With the purchase of your electric pressure cooker, you've entered the world of easy, quick and delicious meals! With minimal preparation and the push of a button, you can create savory main dishes, tempting vegetables, satisfying rice, whole grain dishes, and even delectable desserts. It's easy to understand why today, more than ever, electric pressure cookers are the new favorite kitchen appliance of busy cooks across the nation.

When asked to name a food that cooks in a pressure cooker, most people automatically list traditionally favorite foods, such as stews, pot roast and ribs. But, the world of pressure cooking is much larger than that! Your pressure cooker offers meals in literally just minutes – during any season of the year. From comforting, hearty soups and stews in the winter and lamb chops or veal in the spring, to chicken salads and ribs in the summer and fast one-dish dinners in the fall, your electric pressure cooker will do it all…in a snap.

The recipes inside this cookbook have been created for your electric pressure cooker and are designed to be easy and fun to prepare. Although cooking times are listed, the actual time may vary so always check to determine that foods are properly cooked. Pork and poultry should register at least 180°F when using a meat thermometer and beef and fish should be cooked according to your preference.

One of the best features of your electric pressure cooker is that foods retain more nutrients than when cooked using other methods. Be sure to select fresh fruit and vegetables, choice cuts of meat and other high-quality groceries to maximize the nutritional goodness of your dishes. Experiment with new flavors, use ingredients with creativity and enjoy the time you'll save in the kitchen as your pressure cooker does all the work for you. Whether it's breakfast, lunch, dinner or dessert, your electric pressure cooker is your new best friend! So, let's get started!

Chapter 2

INVITING APPETIZERS & SNACKS

BBQ MINI
TURKEY MEATBALLS

Serves 10

1 lb.	lean ground turkey
1 cup	soft bread crumbs
2 T.	shallot, minced
¼ t.	salt
¼ t.	black pepper
1 t.	fresh parsley, minced
1 large	egg, beaten
1 T.	extra-virgin olive oil
8 oz.	can tomato sauce
½ cup	water
2 T.	dark brown sugar
2 T.	prepared mustard
1 T.	Worcestershire sauce
1 t.	apple cider vinegar
1 t.	horseradish

In a large bowl, toss together the ground turkey, bread crumbs, shallot, salt, pepper, parsley and beaten egg. Form into walnut-sized meatballs. Place the oil in the removable cooking pot and set to Brown. Add the meatballs and brown on all sides. Discard any excess grease.

In a separate bowl, combine the tomato sauce, water, brown sugar, mustard, Worcestershire sauce, vinegar, and horseradish. Pour the sauce over the browned meatballs and set to High pressure. Cook for 10 minutes. Release the pressure using the quick-release method and remove the lid. To serve, place the meatballs in a serving bowl and serve the sauce on the side.

SHRIMP WITH
SWEET & SOUR SAUCE

Serves 8

1 lb.	medium shrimp, peeled and deveined
¼ lb.	fresh snow peas, washed and ends trimmed
3 T.	soy sauce
2 T.	seasoned rice vinegar
½ cup	fresh pineapple juice
1 T.	sugar
¼ cup	low-sodium chicken broth
	Bibb lettuce leaves arranged on a platter

Combine the shrimp, snow peas, soy sauce, vinegar, juice, sugar and broth in the removable cooking pot. Stir to blend. Set to High pressure and cook for 3 minutes. Use the quick-release method to release the pressure and remove the lid. Place the shrimp on the lettuce leaves and pour the remaining sauce into a small bowl. Serve the sauce with the shrimp.

COCONUT CURRY-SAUCED CHICKEN WINGS

Serves 8

⅔ cup	coconut, shredded
1½ cups	plain yogurt
2 lbs.	chicken wing drumettes
2 T.	toasted sesame oil
½ cup	salted peanuts, coarsely chopped

Place the coconut in a shallow pan and the plain yogurt in separate bowl. Dip the chicken wings into the plain yogurt, then dredge each in the coconut. Place the sesame oil in the removable cooking pot and set to Brown. Place the wings in the oil and brown evenly for 10 minutes, turning as the wings brown. When done, the meat should be cooked through with no pink remaining. Remove with a slotted spoon. To serve, place the wings on a serving plate and sprinkle with the chopped peanuts.

HONEY MUSTARD
LAMB RIBLETS

Serves 8

½ cup	vegetable oil
¼ cup	Worcestershire sauce
2 cloves	garlic, crushed
¾ cup	soy sauce
2 T.	dry mustard
1 T.	honey
1 t.	ground black pepper
1 T.	fresh parsley, minced
⅓ cup	lemon juice
2½ lbs.	lamb riblets, cut into individual pieces

Combine all of the ingredients in a self-sealing plastic bag. Mix thoroughly, seal, and refrigerate for 4 to 24 hours. Place the riblets and the marinade in the removable cooking pot. Set to High pressure and cook 10 to 15 minutes. Release the pressure using the quick-release method and remove the lid. Remove the riblets and serve while warm.

BUBBLY PEPPER JACK
CHEESE DIP

Serves 8

1 T.	vegetable oil
¼ cup	yellow onion, minced
½ cup	half and half cream
1 T.	ground cumin
½ t.	salt
2 cups	pepper Jack cheese, shredded

Place the oil in the removable cooking pot and set to Brown. Add the onion and sauté until soft. Add the cream, cumin and salt and whisk constantly as the half and half begins to heat. Do not allow the cream to boil. When the cream starts to form small bubbles, set to Warm and quickly add the cheese. Continue stirring until the cheese is completely melted. Pour the cheese dip into a heatproof bowl and provide fresh vegetables and chips to dip.

CABBAGE & SHIITAKE
MUSHROOM DUMPLINGS

Serves 10

6 small	**shiitake mushrooms, stems discarded, minced**
½ lb.	**ground lean pork**
¼ lb.	**medium-size shrimp, shelled, deveined, finely chopped**
¼ cup	**green onion, minced**
2 T.	**soy sauce**
I clove	**garlic, minced**
I t.	**ground ginger**
½ lb.	**pkg. wonton wrappers**
2 whole	**cabbage leaves**

Condiments:
small bowls of fish sauce, soy sauce, red chile sauce and chopped peanuts

In a large bowl, combine the mushrooms, pork, shrimp, green onion, soy sauce, garlic and ginger. Place a rounded teaspoon of the filling in the center of each wonton wrapper, dab the edges of the wrapper with water, and twist the corners together to make a sealed pocket. Pour I cup of water into the removable cooking pot and place a steamer rack* inside. Layer the cabbage leaves on the rack and place several dumplings on the cabbage leaves. (You will need to steam in batches.) Cover and set to Steam. Steam for 8 to 10 minutes, or until the wrappers are very tender and the shrimp is fully cooked. Serve with small bowls of condiments.

You can find a steamer rack or an expandable steaming basket at many grocery and kitchen specialty stores.

Chilled Vinaigrette
Brussels Sprouts

Serves 10 to 12

6 slices	smoked bacon
1 ¼ lbs.	fresh Brussels sprouts
⅓ cup	vegetable oil
3 T.	white wine vinegar
½ cup	water chestnuts, sliced
2 T.	green onions, thinly sliced
	salt and ground black pepper to taste

Place the bacon in the removable cooking pot and set to Brown. Turn the bacon occasionally until crisp. Remove to a paper towel to drain and crumble. Add the Brussels sprouts to the bacon grease and quickly sauté. Discard any excess grease and add 1 cup water to the sprouts. Set to High pressure and cook for 3 to 4 minutes. Release the pressure using the quick-release method and remove the lid.

Spoon the Brussels sprouts into a serving bowl. In a small bowl, whisk together the oil, wine vinegar, water chestnuts, green onions, crumbled bacon, salt and pepper. Pour the dressing over the Brussels sprouts and toss well to coat. Serve hot or cover and chill for 4 hours.

Asian Shredded
Beef Pockets

Serves 12

¼ cup	soy sauce
3 T.	rice vinegar
3 T.	fresh ginger, minced
2 cloves	garlic, minced
2½ lbs.	beef roast, boneless, trimmed of excess fat
1 cup	low-sodium chicken broth
1 cup	green cabbage, shredded
6	pita bread rounds, cut in half
½ cup	creamy horseradish
1½ cups	green onions, thinly sliced

In a self-sealing plastic bag, combine the soy sauce, vinegar, ginger, garlic and the roast, and coat the meat thoroughly with the marinade. Refrigerate for 4 to 6 hours. Place the roast in the removable cooking pot and add the chicken broth and any remaining marinade to the cooker. Set to High pressure. Cook for 45 to 50 minutes or until the meat shreds easily. Release the pressure using the quick-release method and remove the lid.

Place the meat on a board, let stand 10 minutes and then shred. Set the cooking pot to Brown and heat the remaining meat juices. Add the cabbage and cook just until it wilts, about 5 minutes. To make the pocket sandwiches, spread the inside of each pita with creamy horseradish and fill with some of the wilted cabbage. Add the shredded meat and top with green onions.

SUN-DRIED TOMATO
HUMMUS DIP

Serves 8 to 10

2 T.	extra-virgin olive oil
1 clove	garlic, minced
¼ cup	white onion, minced
2 15 oz.	cans garbanzo beans, rinsed and drained
1 t.	tahini (sesame paste)
3 T.	sun-dried tomatoes packed in oil
	salt and pepper to taste
10	black olives, pitted and chopped
¼ cup	feta cheese, crumbled

Place the oil in the removable cooking pot and set to Brown. Add the garlic and onion and sauté until the vegetables are softened. Add the garbanzo beans, tahini, sun-dried tomatoes and salt and pepper to taste. Heat and stir until the flavors are well-combined. Using a food processor or blender, remove half of the beans and vegetables and purée. Repeat with the remaining half of the beans and vegetables. Return all of the puréed beans to the cooking pot and add the black olives and feta cheese. Continue stirring and cooking for 1 to 3 minutes, or until the cheese is slightly melted and the hummus is warm throughout. Serve with pita chips or pita bread triangles.

Chapter 3

DELIGHTFUL BREAKFASTS, BRUNCHES & LUNCHES

Yukon Gold Potatoes with Havarti Dill Eggs & Bacon

Serves 4

4 strips	smoked bacon, un-cooked
5	medium Yukon Gold potatoes, washed and cut into 1-inch pieces
½ cup	yellow onion, chopped
4 large	eggs, beaten (or egg substitute)
1 t.	black pepper
½ t.	salt
2 t.	fresh dill, minced
4 oz.	Havarti dill cheese, shredded (you may substitute Monterey Jack cheese)

Place the bacon in the removable cooking pot and set to Brown. Cook and stir until crispy and browned. Remove and cool. Reserve 1 tablespoon of the bacon grease and discard the remaining grease. Place the potatoes in the removable cooking pot and add 1 cup of water. Set the cooker to High pressure and cook for 4 minutes.

When done, use the quick-release method to release the pressure and remove the lid. Drain the potatoes and return them to the cooking pot. Layer the onions over the potatoes and pour the eggs over all. Cover with the pepper and salt. Sprinkle the dill over the eggs and add the cheese and bacon. Set to Brown. Cook for 3 minutes. Use a plastic spatula to lift and turn the eggs as they cook. Cook for an additional 3 minutes or until the eggs are moist, but set. Serve while warm.

Canadian Trapper Eggs
with Fried Bread

Serves 4

2 T.	extra-virgin olive oil
½	medium purple onion, peeled and cut into thin slices
8 oz.	tube refrigerated crescent rolls, separated
4 large	eggs (or egg substitute)
½ cup	cheddar cheese, shredded
2 oz.	Canadian bacon, diced
½ t.	salt
¼ t.	black pepper

Pour the oil into the removable cooking pot and add the onion slices. Set to Brown. Sauté for 10 to 15 minutes, turning the slices occasionally. Remove the onions as they begin to brown. Set aside. Do not discard the oil.

Place 4 of the flat dough triangles in the cooking pot. Set to Brown and fry for 2 to 3 minutes or until the triangles are browned on the bottom. Turn with a plastic spatula and fry for 2 to 3 minutes. Remove and keep warm. Repeat with the remaining dough. Use a paper towel to wipe out any remaining grease in the cooking pot.

In a medium bowl, beat together the eggs, cheese, bacon, salt and pepper. Pour the eggs into the removable cooking pot and layer the onion slices over all. Set to Brown and cook for 4 to 6 minutes, lifting the edges and cooking the eggs evenly. Remove the eggs when set and invert onto a large serving platter. Cut into 4 wedges and serve with the warm bread.

QUICK & EASY MIGAS
(MEXICAN SCRAMBLED EGGS)

Serves 4

4 large	eggs, lightly beaten
2 T.	fresh mild salsa
2 T.	yellow onion, chopped
¼ cup	red bell pepper, chopped
1	fresh jalapeño pepper, minced (you may substitute ¼ cup canned green chilies, diced)
1 cup	tortilla chips, slightly broken
1 cup	Monterey Jack cheese, shredded
1 t.	fresh cilantro, minced
4	warm flour tortillas

In a large bowl, beat together the eggs, salsa, onion and peppers until well-blended. Pour into the removable cooking pot and set to Brown. Sauté for 3 minutes, turning and scrambling the eggs as they cook. Add the tortilla chips and stir. Cook for 2 to 3 minutes and remove when almost completely set. Add the cheese, stirring to melt the cheese. Garnish with the cilantro and serve with the warm flour tortillas.

SAN FRANCISCO JOE'S EGGS
WITH FRESH SPINACH

Serves 6

1 lb.	lean ground beef
1 cup	yellow onion, diced
1 t.	salt
½ t.	black pepper
6 large	eggs
	(or egg substitute)
1 cup	fresh spinach, washed, drained and chopped
1 t.	fresh marjoram, minced
1 t.	fresh oregano, minced
	sour cream for garnish

Crumble the beef into the removable cooking pot and set to Brown. Cook and stir until the beef is well-browned. Drain any grease. Add the onion, salt and pepper and toss. Beat the eggs and add the spinach, marjoram and oregano. Pour over the beef and scramble, turning and cooking the eggs and spinach for 4 to 5 minutes, or until the eggs are set and warmed throughout. Garnish with the sour cream and serve while warm.

Molasses & Fuji Apple
Oatmeal

Serves 4

2 cups	lowfat milk
1 cup	quick-cooking oats (not instant)
3 T.	dark molasses
¼ t.	salt
½ t.	ground cinnamon
pinch	nutmeg
1	medium Fuji apple, cored and finely chopped (substitute any kind of tart apple)
½ cup	golden raisins

In a large bowl, mix together the milk, oats, molasses, salt, cinnamon and nutmeg. Add the apple and raisins. Pour the oatmeal mixture into the removable cooking pot. Set to Slow Cook and cook for 1 hour, or until the oatmeal is creamy and tender.

GOLDEN ONION SOUP WITH HOMEMADE CROUTONS

Serves 6

2 T.	butter or margarine
2	medium yellow onions, peeled and thinly sliced
½ cup	sherry
8 cups	beef broth
1	bay leaf
½ t.	salt
½ t.	black pepper
½ loaf	French bread, crust removed, cut into small cubes
¼ cup	butter or margarine, melted
1½ cups	Gruyere cheese, shredded (you may substitute Swiss cheese)

Place the butter in the removable cooking pot and add the sliced onions. Set to Brown and sauté for 10 minutes, or until the onions are golden. Add the sherry, broth, bay leaf, salt and pepper. Set to Steam and steam for 10 minutes.

Meanwhile, place the bread cubes on a baking sheet and drizzle with the melted butter. Broil in the oven for 3 minutes, turn and continue broiling until the croutons are crispy. Remove and cool.

Place equal portions of the Gruyere cheese in 6 individual bowls. Ladle the hot soup over the cheese and add croutons to each serving.

Fresh Asian Noodle Soup
with Vegetables

40 oz.	low-sodium chicken broth (6 cups)
2 T.	soy sauce
8 oz.	fresh thin-cut Asia noodles (sold in produce dept. of grocery store)
1 t.	sesame oil
½ t.	red chile oil
½ cup	fresh carrots, peeled and cut into thin pieces
½ cup	fresh sugar snap peas, washed and trimmed
1	medium egg, beaten sliced green onions for garnish

Place the broth and soy sauce in the removable cooking pot. Stir and add the fresh noodles, sesame oil, red chile oil, carrots and peas. Set to High pressure and cook for 4 minutes. Use the quick-release method to release the pressure and remove the lid. Slowly pour the egg into the soup, forming thin strands. Stir and ladle into bowls. Garnish with the green onions.

Butternut Squash Soup
with Fresh Basil

Serves 3 to 4

2 T.	extra-virgin olive oil
I small	yellow onion, peeled and diced
4 cups	fresh butternut squash, peeled and seeded
½ cup	fresh celery, washed and thinly sliced
4 cups	low-sodium chicken broth
I T.	fresh basil, chopped
I t.	freshly ground black pepper
I t.	salt
I cup	half and half cream

Pour the oil into the removable cooking pot and add the onion. Set to Brown and cook for 2 to 3 minutes or until the onions are tender. Add the squash, celery, chicken broth, basil, pepper and salt and stir to combine. Set to High pressure and cook for 4 minutes. Use the quick-release method to release the pressure and remove the lid.

Pour one-half of the soup into a blender and purée. Repeat with the remaining half. Pour all of the soup back into the cooking pot and add the cream. Set to Brown and stir occasionally until the soup is thickened and warm throughout. Add salt and pepper to taste. Serve while warm.

THICK & HEARTY
MINESTRONE SOUP

Serves 4 to 5

1 T.	extra-virgin olive oil
1	medium yellow onion, peeled and diced
½ cup	celery, chopped
2	fresh carrots, peeled and sliced
½ head	green cabbage, cored and thickly sliced
1 t.	ground oregano
½ t.	ground thyme
2 cloves	garlic, minced
2 t.	salt
1 t.	black pepper
2 cups	water
4 cups	low-sodium chicken broth
16 oz.	canned cannellini beans, rinsed and drained
½ cup	barley, uncooked
1 cup	fresh green beans, trimmed into 1-inch pieces
1½ cups	small pasta shells, uncooked
	freshly grated Parmesan cheese for garnish

Pour the oil into the removable cooking pot and set to Brown. Add the onion, celery and carrots. Sauté for 3 to 4 minutes, stirring occasionally. Add all of the remaining ingredients except the Parmesan cheese, and stir well to combine. Set to High pressure and cook for 6 minutes. Use the quick-release method to release the pressure and remove the lid. Ladle into bowls and garnish each serving with Parmesan cheese.

PULLED PORK SANDWICHES
WITH ZESTY BARBECUE MOP

Serves 6

2 lbs.	pork tenderloin
2 cups	beef broth
1 t.	salt
½ t.	black pepper
2 T.	yellow onion, chopped
16 oz.	can tomato sauce
1 T.	spicy mustard
2 T.	dark brown sugar
1 T.	Worcestershire sauce
6	soft hoagie or ciabatta rolls, split

Place the pork in the removable cooking pot and set to Brown. Sauté the pork, turning occasionally until the pork is browned on all sides. Add the beef broth, salt, pepper and onions and set to High pressure. Cook for 40 minutes. Use the quick-release method to release the pressure and remove the lid. Use a meat thermometer to check that the internal temperature of the pork is 170-175°F. If not, bring to High pressure and continue cooking for 5 to 10 minutes. Release the pressure again and remove the pork. Discard the remaining liquid. Pull the pork into shreds.

Place the tomato sauce, mustard, brown sugar and Worcestershire sauce in the cooking pot and set to Brown. Stir and cook the sauce for 4 to 5 minutes, or until it is warm throughout and the sugar is melted. Add the shredded pork. To serve, spoon the pork and sauce onto half of the rolls and top with the remaining halves. Serve the remaining sauce on the side.

Chicken, Blue Cheese & Tart Apple Salad

Serves 4

2	boneless, skinless chicken breasts
I cup	water
2	medium tart apples, cored and cut into bite-sized pieces
½ cup	walnut halves
½ cup	celery, chopped
¼ t.	black pepper
¼ t.	salt
3 oz.	blue cheese, crumbled
½ cup	lowfat mayonnaise
2 T.	lowfat milk

Place the chicken breasts in the removable cooking pot and add the water. Set to High pressure and cook for 6 minutes. Use the quick-release method to release the pressure and remove the lid. It is done when no pink remains and the internal temperature of the meat is 180°F when tested with a thermometer. If the chicken is not done, return to High pressure and cook for 2 to 3 minutes. Cool and cut the chicken into bite-sized pieces.

In a large serving bowl, combine the chicken, apples, walnuts and celery. Blend together the pepper, salt, blue cheese, mayonnaise and milk. Pour over the chicken salad and toss until all ingredients are coated. Chill for up to 1 hour and serve.

TEX-MEX CHICKEN SALAD WITH CREAMY CILANTRO DRESSING

Serves 4

2	boneless, skinless chicken breasts
I cup	water
I cup	fresh or frozen corn kernels
½ cup	green bell pepper, chopped
I cup	canned small white beans, rinsed and drained
2	Roma tomatoes, chopped
¼ cup	white onion, chopped

Cilantro Dressing:

2 T.	fresh cilantro, chopped
I T.	lowfat milk
¼ cup	lowfat mayonnaise
¼ cup	lowfat sour cream
2 T.	lime juice
¼ t.	chili powder

Place the chicken breasts in the removable cooking pot and add the water. Set to High pressure and cook for 6 minutes. Use the quick-release method to release the pressure and remove the lid. It is done when no pink remains and the internal temperature of the meat is 180°F when tested with a thermometer. If the chicken is not done, return to High pressure and cook for 2 to 3 minutes. Cool and cut the chicken into bite-sized pieces.

In a large serving bowl, combine the chicken, corn, pepper, beans, tomatoes and onion and toss. Mix together the *Cilantro Dressing* and pour over the salad. Chill for up to 2 hours or serve at once.

VIETNAMESE NOODLE SALAD
WITH PEANUT DRESSING

Serves 4

¼ cup	creamy peanut butter
3 T.	soy sauce
3 T.	rice vinegar
¼ cup	peanut oil
I T.	sesame oil
I t.	red chile oil
2 T.	sugar
2	boneless, skinless chicken breasts, cut into bite-sized pieces
4 oz.	fresh Asian wide-cut noodles
6 cups	water
2	green onions, sliced
2 T.	roasted peanuts, chopped

In a medium bowl, whisk together the peanut butter, soy sauce, vinegar, oils and sugar. Set aside.

Place the chicken and fresh noodles in the removable cooking pot and add the water. Set to High pressure and cook for 5 minutes. Use the quick-release method to release the pressure and remove the lid. It is done when no pink remains. If the chicken is not done, return to High pressure and cook for 2 minutes. When done, drain the noodles and chicken and cool.

In a serving bowl, combine the chicken and noodles with the peanut dressing and toss lightly. Add the green onions and peanuts and toss again. Serve while warm or chill for up to I hour.

BAKED POTATO SOUP
WITH TOPPINGS

Serves 4

4 slices	smoked bacon
4 large	russet potatoes, peeled and cut into quarters
½ cup	white onions, chopped
4 cups	low-sodium chicken broth
I t.	salt
½ t.	black pepper
I cup	heavy cream

Toppings:
chopped green onions or chives,
shredded cheddar cheese,
prepared salsa,
steamed broccoli,
sour cream or butter

Place the bacon in the removable cooking pot and set to Brown. Sauté and stir for 6 minutes or until the bacon is crisp. Set aside to drain on a paper towel. Place the potatoes in the cooking pot and add the onions, broth, salt and pepper. Set to High pressure and cook for 5 minutes. Use the quick-release method to release the pressure and remove the lid.

For a creamy texture, use a blender to process the soup in batches until smooth and return to the pot. Set to Brown and when the soup is hot, slowly add the cream, stirring constantly. Adjust the seasonings to your taste, add the bacon, and serve with the toppings.

Thirty Minute
Split Pea Soup

Serves 4 to 6

4 slices	bacon, chopped
I large	yellow onion, peeled and chopped
3	carrots, peeled and chopped
3	new potatoes, washed and chopped
I cup	dried split peas, sorted and rinsed
3 cups	chicken broth
I	bay leaf
I t.	salt
½ t.	black pepper croutons for garnish

Place the bacon and onions in the removable cooking pot and set to Brown. Sauté the bacon and onions, stirring occasionally. Add the carrots, potatoes, peas, chicken broth and bay leaf and stir. Add the salt and pepper and stir again. Set to High pressure and cook for 10 minutes. Use the natural-release method to release the pressure and remove the lid. To serve, ladle the soup into bowls and garnish each serving with croutons.

Chapter 4

SATISFYING VEGETABLES, GRAINS & SIDE DISHES

Avocado & Brown Rice
Salad

Serves 4

1 T.	butter or margarine
1 cup	long grain brown rice, uncooked
2 cups	low-sodium chicken broth
2	medium Haas avocados, cut into ½-inch cubes
¼ cup	fresh Italian parsley, minced
½	cucumber, peeled, seeded and chopped
¼ cup	green onions, chopped
2 T.	fresh lemon juice
1 T.	extra-virgin olive oil
¼ t.	ground black pepper chopped parsley for garnish

Place the butter in the removable cooking pot and set to Brown. Add the brown rice and sauté for 2 to 4 minutes, stirring continually. Add the chicken broth and set to High pressure. Cook for 20 to 25 minutes. Use the quick-release method to release the pressure and remove the lid. Pour the rice into a salad bowl to cool to room temperature.

Place the avocados, parsley, cucumber, green onions, lemon juice, olive oil and black pepper in a bowl and mix gently. Carefully add the avocado and vegetables to the cooled rice. Garnish with the parsley.

Barley, Brown Rice & Bulgur Pilaf

¼ cup	butter or margarine
1 large	white onion, chopped
1 clove	garlic, minced
⅓ cup	walnuts, chopped
⅓ cup	barley
⅓ cup	brown rice
⅓ cup	bulgur
2 cups	chicken or beef broth
2 T.	fresh flat-leaf Italian parsley, chopped
½ t.	fresh basil, minced
½ t.	fresh oregano, minced
½ t.	ground black pepper

Place the butter in the removable cooking pot and set to Brown. Add the onion and garlic and sauté for 2 minutes, stirring occasionally. Add the walnuts, barley, brown rice, and bulgur and sauté for an additional 2 minutes. Add the broth, herbs and black pepper and blend well. Cover and set to High pressure. Cook for 20 minutes. Use the quick-release method to release the pressure and remove the lid. Fluff the grains and spoon into a serving bowl.

Southwest Baked Beans
with Pepper Jack Cheese

Serves 6

2 cups	pinto beans, washed and sorted
½ lb.	bacon
1	medium yellow onion, diced
2 t.	ground chili powder
2 cloves	garlic, minced
¾ cup	firmly packed light brown sugar
12 oz.	bottle dark beer salt and ground black pepper to taste
½ cup	pepper Jack cheese, shredded

Place the beans in a large pot and add enough water to fill the entire pot. Soak the beans overnight. Drain the beans. Place the bacon in the removable cooking pot and set to Brown. Cook and stir the bacon until browned and crisp. Remove the bacon and set aside. Drain off all of the remaining grease except 2 tablespoons. Set to Brown and sauté the onion, chili powder and garlic for 4 minutes. Add the beans and stir. Add water to cover at least 2-inches above the beans. Add the bacon, sugar, beer, salt and pepper. Stir and set to High pressure. Cook for 8 to 10 minutes, or until beans are soft. Use the natural-release method to release the pressure and remove the lid. Garnish with the shredded cheese.

BUTTERMILK
MASHED POTATOES

Serves 4

4	medium russet potatoes, peeled and cut into quarters
2 cloves	garlic, crushed
1 cup	water
¼ cup	butter or margarine
½ t.	salt
¼ t.	ground black pepper
1 cup	fresh buttermilk

Place the potatoes, garlic and water in the removable cooking pot. Set to High pressure and cook for 5 minutes, or until the potatoes are very tender. Release the pressure using the natural-release method and remove the lid.

Using a slotted spoon, remove the potatoes and garlic from the pot and place in a large mixing bowl. Add the butter, salt and pepper and mash with a fork or potato masher, adding the buttermilk until the potatoes are creamy.

Steamed Summer Fresh
Vegetables with Butter & Basil

Serves 4

2	carrots, peeled, sliced ¼-inch thick
1 cup	celery, sliced
3	green onions, cut into 1-inch pieces
½	green bell pepper, coarsely chopped
2	medium zucchini, sliced 1-inch thick
1	large ripe tomato, cored and cut into eighths
1 T.	fresh basil, chopped
¼ t.	ground black pepper
	salt to taste
2 T.	butter or margarine

Layer the vegetables on a piece of foil. Top the vegetables with the basil, pepper and salt and dot with butter. Tightly close the vegetable foil packet, crimping the edges tightly.

Place 1 cup of water into the removable cooking pot. Place a steamer rack* over the water and place the vegetable packet on the steamer rack. Cover and set to Steam. Steam for 4 to 5 minutes. Carefully remove the vegetable packet and spoon the steamed vegetables into a serving bowl.

*You can find a steamer rack or an expandable steaming basket at many grocery and kitchen specialty stores.

FRENCH GREEN BEANS
WITH CRISPY SHALLOTS

Serves 4 to 6

¼ cup	flour
¼ t.	black pepper, freshly ground
½ t.	salt
8	shallots, white parts only, thinly sliced and separated into rings
¼ cup	vegetable or peanut oil
2 lbs.	French green beans (thin and/or petite green beans), washed and ends trimmed

Combine the flour, pepper and salt in a self-sealing plastic bag. Sprinkle the shallots with water and add one-fourth of the rings to the flour mixture. Shake the shallots until each ring is lightly coated with the flour mixture. Repeat with the remaining rings and set aside.

Place the oil in the removable cooking pot and set to Brown. Add enough shallots to cover the bottom of the pan. Pan fry until crisp and golden. Remove and place on absorbent paper to dry. Repeat with the remaining shallots. Pour out any remaining oil and discard.

Place the green beans on a steamer rack* in the removable cooking pot. Add 1 cup of water. Set to High pressure and cook for 2 minutes. Use the quick-release method to release the pressure and remove the lid. To serve, mound the green beans on a serving platter and top with the crispy shallots. Serve at once.

*You can find a steamer rack or an expandable steaming basket at many grocery and kitchen specialty stores.

| Chapter 4 SATISFYING VEGETABLES, GRAINS & SIDE DISHES

SESAME BROCCOLI
RABE

Serves 4

1 lb.	broccoli rabe, cleaned and separated
1 T.	extra-virgin olive oil
1 T.	balsamic vinegar
1 T.	soy sauce
1 T.	sugar
1 T.	toasted sesame seeds

Pour 1 cup of water into the removable cooking pot. Place a steamer rack* over the water. Place the rabe on the rack and set to Steam. Steam 5 to 7 minutes, or until the rabe is tender-crisp.

In a small saucepan, heat the olive oil, vinegar, soy sauce, sugar and sesame seeds until gently simmering. Place the rabe in a shallow bowl and dress it with the hot sesame seed sauce to coat. Serve immediately.

*You can find a steamer rack or an expandable steaming basket at many grocery and kitchen specialty stores.

Warm D'Anjou
Pear & Apple Salad

Serves 4

2 large	Granny Smith apples, unpeeled, cored and cut into cubes
2 large	D'Angou pears, unpeeled, cored and cut into cubes
1 T.	honey
10 oz.	hearts of romaine lettuce, coarsely chopped
½ cup	roasted pecans, coarsely chopped
¼ cup	dried cranberries
½ cup	plain yogurt
1 t.	prepared horseradish
1 t.	lemon juice
dash	ground black pepper

Place 1 cup of water in the removable cooking pot. Add a steamer rack* and place the apples and pears on the rack. Drizzle the honey over the fruit. Set to Steam. Steam for 4 to 6 minutes, or until the fruit is just tender. Remove the fruit and cool slightly.

In a large salad bowl, combine the lettuce, pecans and cranberries. In a small bowl, make the dressing by whisking together the yogurt, horseradish, lemon juice and a dash of pepper. Add the steamed fruit to the lettuce and toss all together with the dressing. Serve immediately.

You can find a steamer rack or an expandable steaming basket at many grocery and kitchen specialty stores.

WALNUT-STUFFED
ACORN SQUASH WITH HERBS

Serves 2 to 3

½ cup	toasted walnuts, chopped
½ small	yellow onion, minced
¼ t.	dried oregano
I T.	fresh parsley, minced
¼ t.	ground black pepper
¼ cup	soft bread crumbs
I large	egg, beaten
I	acorn squash, cut in half lengthwise, seeds removed

Pour I cup of water into the removable cooking pot. Place a steamer rack* in the cooking pot. In a small bowl, combine all of the ingredients except the squash. Spoon even amounts of the stuffing mix into each squash half and place the halves in the cooking pot. If large, the halves may be pressed side by side. Cover and set to Steam. Steam for 40 to 45 minutes, or until the squash is tender. To serve, slice the squash into wedges.

You can find a steamer rack or an expandable steaming basket at many grocery and kitchen specialty stores.

Fresh Vegetables with Dijon Dressing

Serves 4

¼ lb.	**fresh asparagus, cut in 1½-inch pieces**
2 cups	**fresh carrots, cut into ¼-inch slices**
8 oz.	**fresh green beans, cut in 1½-inch pieces**
4 oz.	**fresh mushrooms, cleaned and quartered**
2	**medium ripe red tomatoes, cored and cut into wedges**
¼ cup	**fresh shallot, diced**

Dijon Dressing:

¼ cup	**plain lowfat yogurt**
2 T.	**rice vinegar**
3 T.	**extra-virgin olive oil**
1 T.	**Dijon mustard**
¼ t.	**ground black pepper**
1 T.	**fresh parsley, minced**

Pour 1 cup of water into the removable cooking pot. Place a steamer rack* in the bottom of the pot. Place the asparagus, carrots and fresh green beans on the rack. Set to Steam and steam for 3 to 4 minutes, or until the vegetables are tender-crisp. Place the vegetables quickly in a large bowl of iced water to stop the cooking process. Spoon the vegetables into a serving bowl and add the mushroom, tomatoes and shallot.

In a small bowl, make the dressing by whisking together the yogurt, vinegar, olive oil, mustard, black pepper and parsley. Toss the vegetables with the dressing and chill for at least 2 hours before serving.

You can find a steamer rack or an expandable steaming basket at many grocery and kitchen specialty stores.

BACON-DRIZZLED
BABY BOK CHOY

Serves 8

6 slices	bacon, uncooked
12 oz.	baby bok choy heads, about 2-inches at the base, ends trimmed
1 cup	water
1 T.	sugar
¼ cup	white vinegar
1 T.	dry mustard

Place the bacon in the removable cooking pot and set to Brown. Sauté the bacon until crispy. Remove the bacon, cool and crumble. Add the bok choy to the bacon drippings in the cooker and stir fry briefly. Remove the bok choy and place on a steamer rack.*

Discard any oil and wipe out the pot with a paper towel. Pour 1 cup of water into the cooking pot, place the steamer rack with the bok choy into the pot and set to Steam. Steam until the bok choy is just tender, about 3 minutes. Remove to a platter. In a small bowl, make the dressing by whisking together the sugar, vinegar, dry mustard and crumbled bacon. Drizzle over the steamed bok choy.

*You can find a steamer rack or an expandable steaming basket at many grocery and kitchen specialty stores.

ITALIAN-HERBED
ARTICHOKES

Serves 2

2	**medium artichokes, cleaned, stems trimmed**
4 T.	**extra-virgin olive oil**
½ t.	**garlic salt**
½ t.	**dried oregano**
½ t.	**dried parsley**
¼ t.	**dried basil**
¼ t.	**ground black pepper**

Pour 1 cup of water into the removable cooking pot and place the two artichokes into the water, stem-side down. Evenly drizzle the oil over the artichokes, then sprinkle each one with the herbs. Set to High pressure and cook for 8 to 10 minutes. Use the quick-release method to release the pressure and remove the lid. Use a slotted spoon to place the artichokes on individual plates.

Black Bean Soup
with Lime & Sour Cream

Serves 4 to 6

2 cups	black beans, sorted and rinsed
4 cups	vegetable broth
3 stalks	celery, chopped fine
2 T.	vegetable oil
I cup	white onion, chopped fine
I	green bell pepper, cored and minced
¼ t.	ground black pepper
2 T.	lime juice, divided
½ cup	sour cream

Soak the beans overnight in a full pot of water. Drain. Place the beans, vegetable broth, oil, celery, onion, green bell pepper and black pepper in the removable cooking pot. Set to High pressure. Cook for 15 to 20 minutes, or until the beans are extremely soft. Release the pressure using the natural-release method and remove the lid. Immediately, pour half of the soup into a blender and purée, adding half of the lime juice. Repeat with the remaining soup and juice. Serve hot with sour cream on top of each serving.

CREAMY POTATO & CARROT SOUP

Serves 4

2 T.	vegetable oil
1	medium yellow onion, diced
1 clove	garlic, minced
3 large	russet potatoes, peeled, thinly sliced
4 large	carrots, peeled, thinly sliced
4 cups	chicken broth
1 t.	ground cumin
1 T.	fresh flat-leaf Italian parsley, minced
½ cup	heavy cream

Place the oil in the removable cooking pot and set to Brown. Add the onion and garlic and sauté for 3 minutes. Add the potatoes, carrots, chicken broth and cumin and stir. Cover and set to High pressure. Cook for 5 minutes. Use the quick-release method to release the pressure and remove the lid. Using a long-handled plastic spoon, break up the carrots and potatoes into very small pieces. Set to Brown and add the parsley and heavy cream. Stir and cook until the soup just begins to bubble. Turn to Warm. Serve in individual bowls.

Mushroom & White Wine
Risotto

Serves 4 to 6

2 T.	extra-virgin olive oil
3 T.	shallots, minced
8 oz.	button mushrooms, coarsely chopped
2 cups	Arborio rice, un-cooked
3 cups	chicken broth
1 cup	dry white wine
¼ cup	Parmesan cheese, freshly grated

Pour the oil into the removable cooking pot and add the shallots. Sauté the shallots just until tender, not brown. Add the mushrooms and rice and cook and stir for 2 minutes. Add the broth and white wine and stir again. Cover and set to High pressure. Cook for 20 to 25 minutes. Release the pressure using the quick-release method and remove the lid. If the rice has not completely cooked, set to High pressure and cook for 5 to 10 minutes. Stir the rice thoroughly, adding the Parmesan cheese to blend. Serve immediately.

SWEET VIDALIA ONION
& AVOCADO PILAF

Serves 6

¼ cup	butter
1 clove	garlic, crushed
½ cup	Vidalia onions, peeled and minced (substitute any sweet onion)
1¼ cups	white mushrooms, sliced
1 cup	long grain white rice, uncooked
1½ cups	chicken broth
¼ cup	dry white wine
2	medium ripe tomatoes, peeled, seeded, and diced
1 t.	dried oregano
¼ t.	ground black pepper
2 T.	fresh flat-leaf Italian parsley, minced
1	ripe Haas avocado, peeled and diced
1 T.	lemon juice

Place the butter in the removable cooking pot and set to Brown. Add the garlic, onions and mushrooms and sauté for 3 minutes. Add the white rice and sauté for 3 to 4 minutes. Add the chicken broth, white wine, tomatoes, oregano, black pepper and parsley. Stir and set to High pressure. Cook for 20 to 25 minutes. Use the quick-release method to release the pressure and remove the lid. Stir and fluff the rice and spoon into a serving bowl. In a small bowl, combine the avocado with the lemon juice and toss it gently with the rice. Serve immediately.

RASPBERRY VINAIGRETTE
LENTIL SALAD

Serves 6 to 8

1 ½ cups	dried lentils, cleaned and sorted
3 cups	chicken broth
⅓ cup	vegetable oil
2 T.	raspberry vinegar or wine vinegar
2 T.	fresh shallot, minced
2 t.	Dijon mustard
¼ t.	ground black pepper
3 T.	capers
2	medium tomatoes, firm-ripe, coarsely chopped

Place the lentils and chicken broth in the removable cooking pot. Set to High pressure and cook for 8 to 10 minutes, or until the lentils are tender. Use the quick-release method to release the pressure and remove the lid. Drain off any excess liquid and cool the lentils slightly. In a small bowl, whisk together the vegetable oil, vinegar, shallot, mustard and black pepper to make the dressing. In a large salad bowl, combine the cooled lentils, capers, and tomatoes and gently toss with the dressing. Serve at room temperature.

Chapter 5

SAVORY POULTRY & SEAFOOD ENTRÉES

Green-Chile
Chicken Paella

Serves 4

2 T.	extra-virgin olive oil
1	medium white onion, peeled and chopped
¼ cup	green bell pepper, cored and chopped
4 oz.	can chopped green chilies
3	chicken thighs, boneless, skinless, cut into bite-sized pieces
3 oz.	smoked chicken sausage, diced
3 cups	chicken broth
1 cup	long grain white rice, uncooked
1 cup	canned white shoepeg corn (you may substitute yellow corn)
2 t.	smoked ground paprika (you may substitute regular paprika)
1 t.	ground chili powder
pinch	saffron threads
8	soft flour tortillas, warmed

Pour the olive oil into the removable cooking pot and set to Brown. Sauté the onion, green pepper and chilies in the oil until softened and translucent. Add the chicken and continue sautéing until the chicken pieces are browned, about 3 minutes.

Add the sausage, broth, rice, corn, paprika, chili powder and saffron threads and stir to mix. Set to High pressure and cook for 20 to 25 minutes. Use the quick-release method to release the pressure and remove the lid. To serve, divide the paella among four plates and garnish with additional paprika, if desired. Serve with the warmed tortillas.

Quick Chicken, Tomatoes & Peppers with Linguine

Serves 4

3 lbs.	fryer chicken, cut into pieces
1 T.	sweet Hungarian paprika
2 T.	extra-virgin olive oil, divided
1 large	red onion, peeled and finely sliced
1	green bell pepper, cored and thickly sliced
14.5 oz.	can diced tomatoes with juice
½ cup	chicken broth
8 oz.	linguine pasta, cooked al dente and kept warm

Season the chicken pieces with the paprika. Place 1 tablespoon of oil in the removable cooking pot and set to Brown. Add the onion slices and sauté just until tender, but not brown. Remove the onion, add the remaining olive oil and brown the chicken, turning to brown the pieces on all sides. Add the remaining ingredients except the linguine and stir. Set to High pressure and cook for 10 to 12 minutes. Release the pressure using the quick-release method and remove the lid. Serve the chicken and sauce over the warm linguine.

CORNISH GAME HEN
FOR TWO

Serves 2

2 T.	butter or margarine
1	medium white onion, peeled and sliced
1½ lbs.	Cornish game hen
1 cup	low-sodium chicken broth
½ cup	sauterne or white cooking wine
1 T.	Dijon mustard
1 T.	fresh basil, minced
6	medium whole mushrooms, cleaned and sliced

Place the butter in the removable cooking pot and set to Brown. Add the onion slices and sauté for 3 minutes. Add the Cornish game hen and brown on all sides. In a small bowl, whisk together the chicken broth, wine, mustard and basil. Pour over the game hen, add the mushrooms and set to High pressure. Cook for 12 to 15 minutes. Use the quick-release method to release the pressure and remove the lid. To serve, cut the hen in half at the breast bone. Spoon the mushrooms over each serving.

LIME CHICKEN WITH JAMAICAN RUM SAUCE

Serves 4

8 oz.	can unsweetened pineapple chunks, drained, juice reserved
½ cup	dark Jamaican rum
3 T.	lime juice
2 T.	soy sauce
1 T.	brown sugar
2 cloves	garlic, minced
2 t.	ground curry powder
½ t.	ground ginger
¼ t.	ground cloves
¼ t.	red cayenne pepper
4	chicken breast halves, boneless, skinless
11 oz.	can mandarin orange segments, drained

In a self-sealing plastic bag combine the reserved pineapple juice, rum, lime juice, soy sauce, brown sugar, garlic, curry, ginger, cloves and red pepper. Add the chicken breasts and mix to coat well. Refrigerate overnight. Place the chicken and the marinade in the removable cooking pot and set to High pressure. Cook for 8 to 10 minutes, or until a meat thermometer registers 180°F when tested in the thickest part of the chicken. Release the pressure using the quick-release method and remove the lid. Add the mandarin oranges and the pineapple chunks to the chicken and stir to warm. Strain the remaining juices and serve as a sauce with the chicken.

Chicken Breasts with
Marinated Artichoke Brown Rice

Serves 2

2 T.	extra-virgin olive oil
I clove	garlic, minced
I	medium shallot, minced
2	chicken breasts, bone-in, skinless
½ cup	brown rice, uncooked
I cup	chicken broth
7.5 oz.	jar marinated artichoke hearts, undrained, chopped
2 T.	pine nuts

Place the olive oil in the removable cooking pot and set to Brown. Add the garlic and shallot and sauté until tender. Add the chicken breasts and brown on both sides. Remove the browned chicken and add the brown rice. Sauté for 2 minutes. Add the chicken broth and marinated artichokes hearts and blend. Place the chicken breasts on top of the rice. Set to High pressure and cook for 20 to 25 minutes. Use the quick-release method to release the pressure and remove the lid. Fluff the rice and garnish the chicken with the pine nuts.

SOUTHWEST
PUEBLO STEW

Serves 4

2 T.	extra-virgin olive oil
I large	white onion, peeled and coarsely chopped
2 cloves	garlic, minced
I T.	ground chili powder
I t.	ground cumin
¼ t.	ground black pepper
I lb.	chicken breast, boneless, skinless, cut into 1-inch chunks
3	medium zucchini, cut into 1-inch chunks
14 oz.	can chopped tomatoes, undrained
2 16 oz.	cans pinto beans, rinsed and drained
2 cups	chicken broth
I T.	fresh cilantro, minced

Place the olive oil in the removable cooking pot and set to Brown. Add the onion and sauté for I minute. Add the garlic and the spices and sauté for an additional 2 minutes. Add the chicken and brown, turning once to brown both sides. Add the zucchini, tomatoes, beans and broth. Set to High pressure and cook for 10 to12 minutes. Use the quick-release method to release the pressure and remove the lid. Garnish with cilantro to serve.

Note: You may also set to Slow Cook for 8 to 9 hours.

CHICKEN
TORTELLINI SOUP

Serves 4

2 T.	extra-virgin olive oil
1 lb.	chicken breast, boneless, skinless, cut into ½-inch chunks
4 oz.	white mushrooms, cleaned and sliced
½ cup	long grain white rice, uncooked
4 cups	chicken broth
1 cup	dry white wine
2 t.	fresh tarragon, minced
8 oz.	pkg. cheese-filled tortellini
½ cup	Monterey Jack cheese, shredded

Place the olive oil in the removable cooking pot and set to Brown. Add the chicken pieces and brown on all sides. Discard any excess oil. Add the mushrooms, rice, chicken broth, wine, tarragon and tortellini. Set to High pressure and cook for 10 to 15 minutes. Release the pressure using the quick-release method and remove the lid. To serve, ladle into individual bowls and garnish with the cheese.

Glazed Honey & Currant Chicken

Serves 4

½ cup	sweet red wine
½ cup	white vinegar
I cup	currant preserves
2 T.	soy sauce
2 T.	honey
I t.	Dijon mustard
2-3 lbs.	fryer chicken, skinless, cut into pieces

In a self-sealing plastic bag combine the wine, vinegar, preserves, soy sauce, honey and mustard. Blend to combine. Add the chicken pieces and coat thoroughly. Marinate in the refrigerator for 4 to 6 hours.

Place the chicken and marinade into the removable cooking pot and set to High pressure. Cook for 10 to 12 minutes. Use the quick-release method to release the pressure and remove the lid. Serve while warm, spooning the sauce over the chicken.

LEMON CHICKEN
WITH JASMINE RICE

Serves 4

2 T.	extra-virgin olive oil
4 cloves	garlic, minced
2 lbs.	chicken thighs, boneless, skinless
1 cup	chicken broth
¼ cup	fresh lemon juice
3 T.	sugar
4 slices	fresh lemon, peeled
1 T.	cornstarch
2 T.	water
4 cups	jasmine rice, cooked and kept warm

Place the olive oil in the removable cooking pot and set to Brown. Sauté the garlic, add the chicken thighs and brown on all sides. Add the chicken broth, lemon juice, sugar and lemon slices. Cover and set to High pressure. Cook for 8 to 10 minutes, or until the chicken registers 180°F on a meat thermometer. Use the quick-release method to release the pressure and remove the lid. Remove the chicken and keep warm.

Set to Brown and bring the juices to a boil. Stir together the cornstarch and water and add to the boiling sauce, stirring until thickened. To serve, place the chicken on the rice and spoon the lemon sauce over the top.

CRIMINI MUSHROOM-STUFFED
CHICKEN BREASTS

Serves 4

4	crimini mushrooms, minced
¼ cup	panko (Asian) bread-crumbs (substitute dry breadcrumbs if desired)
⅓ cup	fresh Italian parsley, minced
I clove	garlic, minced
⅓ cup	Parmesan cheese, freshly grated
2 T.	chicken broth
4	chicken breast halves, skinless, boneless and pounded thin
2 T.	extra-virgin olive oil
½ cup	chicken broth
½ cup	dry white wine

In a medium bowl, combine the crimini mushrooms, breadcrumbs, parsley, garlic and Parmesan cheese. Place the flattened chicken breasts on a clean surface. Spoon the mushroom mixture onto each piece of chicken. Roll each piece of chicken tightly and tie with cooking string to secure.

Place the olive oil in the removable cooking pot and set to Brown. Add the chicken breasts and brown on all sides. Add the chicken broth and white wine. Set to High pressure. Cook for 11 to 12 minutes, or until the chicken registers 180°F on a meat thermometer. Use the quick-release method to release the pressure and remove the lid. Serve while warm.

Chicken Cacciatore
Over Fettuccini

Serves 4

2 T.	extra-virgin olive oil
1	medium sweet onion, peeled and diced
1 clove	garlic, minced
14 oz.	white mushrooms, cleaned and sliced
2 lbs.	chicken breasts, cut into 2-inch cubes
8 oz.	can tomato sauce
¼ cup	chicken broth
2 T.	fresh basil, chopped
8 oz.	cooked fettuccini noodles, kept warm
	Parmesan cheese, freshly grated

Place the olive oil in the removable cooking pot and set to Brown. Add the onion and garlic and sauté for 2 to 3 minutes. Add the mushrooms and sauté for 3 minutes. Remove the vegetables and add the chicken. Brown the chicken on both sides and add the tomato sauce, chicken broth, sautéed vegetables and fresh basil. Set to High pressure and cook for 10 to 12 minutes, or until the chicken registers 180°F on a meat thermometer. Use the quick-release method to release the pressure and remove the lid. Serve the chicken cacciatore over the cooked pasta and garnish with the Parmesan cheese.

Hot Salsa & Chile
Chicken Soup

Serves 4

2	chicken breast halves, boneless, skinless
3 cups	chicken broth
¼ t.	ground black pepper
2 T.	fresh parsley, minced
1 clove	garlic, minced
1 small	yellow onion, peeled and chopped
½ cup	fresh spicy salsa (substitute mild salsa, if desired)
14.5 oz.	can diced tomatoes with juice
2 t.	ground chili powder
15 oz.	can kernel corn, drained
6 oz.	can sliced olives, drained
4 cups	broken tortilla chips

Place the chicken breasts, chicken broth, black pepper and parsley in the removable cooking pot. Set to High pressure and cook for 8 to 10 minutes, or until the chicken is easily shredded. Use the quick-release method to release the pressure and remove the lid. Remove the chicken to a cutting board and shred. Return the chicken to the juices in the cooking pot and add the other ingredients, except the tortilla chips. Set to High pressure and cook for 5 minutes. Use the quick-release method to release the pressure and remove the lid. Place the tortilla chips in four individual bowls and cover with the soup.

TARRAGON & WHITE WINE
SALMON STEAKS

Serves 3 to 4

1½ lbs.	salmon steaks
1½ cups	white cooking wine
¼ t.	salt
1 t.	fresh tarragon, minced
¼ t.	black pepper
1	lemon, peeled and sliced
	fresh tarragon for garnish

Place the salmon steaks on a steamer rack* in the removable cooking pot. Cover with the wine, salt, tarragon, pepper and lemon slices. Set to High pressure and cook for 6 minutes. Use the quick-release method to release the pressure and remove the lid. Garnish the salmon with the tarragon to serve.

*You can find a steamer rack or an expandable steaming basket at many grocery and kitchen specialty stores.

Sweet Jumbo Shrimp with Snow Peas & Pineapple

Serves 4

1½ lbs.	jumbo shrimp, cleaned and deveined, tails removed
¼ lb.	fresh snow peas, trimmed
1 cup	fresh pineapple, chopped (you may substitute canned pineapple)
2 T.	soy sauce
2 T.	rice vinegar
½ cup	pineapple juice
2 T.	light brown sugar
1 cup	low-sodium chicken broth
1 T.	cornstarch
¼ cup	water
1 T.	soy sauce
2 cups	cooked long grain white rice, kept warm

Place the shrimp, peas and pineapple in the removable cooking pot. Mix together the soy sauce, vinegar, juice, sugar and chicken broth and pour over the shrimp. Set to High pressure and cook for 3 minutes. Use the quick-release method to release the pressure and remove the lid. Remove the shrimp, peas and pineapple from the pot using a slotted spoon. Set aside. Whisk together the cornstarch, water and soy sauce and add to the liquid. Set to Brown and heat, stirring as the mixture thickens. Adjust the seasonings, if desired and add the shrimp, peas and pineapple back to the sauce. Warm briefly and serve over the warm rice.

THAI RED CHILE & COCONUT
SNAPPER

Serves 4

1 lb.	firm red snapper fillets
1 t.	fresh Thai basil, chopped (you may substitute Italian basil)
1 cup	chicken broth
1	dried red chile
1 t.	salt
½ t.	white pepper
1	yellow onion, peeled and chopped
2 cloves	garlic, minced
1 t.	lemon juice
½ cup	coconut milk
2	green onions, chopped

Place the fillets in the removable cooking pot and add the basil and chicken broth. Set to High pressure and cook for 4 to 5 minutes. While the fish cooks, place the red chile, salt, pepper, onion, garlic, lemon juice and coconut milk in a blender and blend until smooth. When the fish is done, use the quick-release method to release the pressure and remove the lid. Remove the fish and all of the broth except ½ cup. Set to Brown and add to the broth the coconut milk and spices along with the green onions. Stir and cook until smooth and return the fillets to the cooker. Heat for 2 minutes and serve.

STEAMED SWEET ONIONS WITH
SHRIMP & WILD RICE STUFFING

Serves 4

4 large	sweet onions, peeled
½ lb.	medium shrimp, peeled and deveined
1 cup	white and wild rice blend, cooked
2 T.	butter, melted
2 T.	chicken broth
2 t.	fresh dill
½ t.	salt
¼ t.	white pepper
	water

Remove all of the inner layers of each onion, leaving a ¼-inch thick shell. In a medium bowl, combine the shrimp, rice, butter, broth, dill, salt and pepper. Stuff each shell with the shrimp and rice mixture. Place the onions on a steamer rack* in the removable cooking pot. Add water to just below the rack. Set to Steam and steam for 10 to 12 minutes. Remove the onions with a slotted spoon.

*You can find a steamer rack or an expandable steaming basket at many grocery and kitchen specialty stores.

CREOLE BOUILLABAISSE

Serves 4 to 6

1 T.	vegetable oil
1 small	yellow onion, peeled and chopped
2 cloves	garlic
1 t.	salt
½ t.	black pepper
1 t.	dried parsley
14.5 oz.	can diced tomatoes, with juice
1	bay leaf
1 t.	dried thyme
½ t.	ground sage
½ t.	Tabasco™ sauce
2 cups	water
2 cups	chicken broth
1 lb.	firm white fish fillets
1 lb.	sea scallops, rinsed
¼ lb.	jumbo shrimp, shelled and deveined
6	baby clams, scrubbed

Place the oil in the removable cooking pot and add the onion and garlic. Set to Brown and sauté until the vegetables are softened. Add the salt, pepper, parsley, tomatoes, bay leaf, thyme, sage, Tabasco sauce, water and chicken broth and blend. Set to High pressure and cook for 5 minutes. Use the quick-release method to release the pressure and remove the lid. Add the fish fillets, scallops, shrimp and clams and set to High pressure. Cook for 3 minutes. Use the quick-release method to release the pressure and remove the lid. Remove the bay leaf and serve while hot.

SEASIDE HARBOR CHOWDER

Serves 4

1 lb.	firm white fish fillets, cut into bite-sized pieces
6	russet potatoes, peeled and cut into bite-sized pieces
1 small	yellow onion, peeled and chopped
1 t.	salt
½ t.	ground white pepper
3 cups	chicken broth
2 cups	half-and-half cream
2 t.	fresh parsley

Place the fillets, potatoes, onion, salt, pepper and chicken broth in the removable cooking pot. Set to High pressure and cook for 6 minutes. Use the quick-release method to release the pressure and remove the lid. Set to Brown and add the cream and parsley, stirring as the soup warms. Continue stirring and cooking for 3 minutes. Do not allow the soup to boil. Serve while warm.

Chapter 6

Hearty Beef, Pork & Lamb Entrées

French Beef Ragout
with Pearl Onions

Serves 4 to 6

2 T.	extra-virgin olive oil
1½ lbs.	beef chuck steak, cut into bite-sized pieces
3 T.	flour
2 cups	fresh pearl onions, peeled (you may substitute frozen onions)
2 cups	carrots, peeled and cut into 1-inch pieces
1 cup	celery, sliced
2	medium russet potatoes, peeled and cut into small pieces
1 T.	fresh basil, minced
1	bay leaf
1 t.	salt
½ t.	black pepper
1 cup	spicy tomato vegetable juice

Pour the oil into the removable cooking pot and set to Brown. Dredge the beef in the flour and place in the cooking pot. Stir occasionally as the beef browns. Sauté until the pieces are browned on each side. Add the remaining ingredients and mix lightly with a spoon. Set to High pressure and cook for 20 minutes. Use the quick-release method to release the pressure and remove the lid. Remove the bay leaf before serving.

RICH BEEF TENDERLOIN WITH
MADEIRA & BLUE CHEESE SAUCE

Serves 6

1 T.	extra-virgin olive oil
2½ lbs.	beef tenderloin, tied
½ t.	black pepper
½ t.	garlic salt
1 cup	water

Madeira & Blue Cheese Sauce:

2 T.	butter or margarine
2 T.	blue cheese, crumbled
½ cup	beef broth
¼ cup	Madeira wine
1 cup	button mushrooms, cleaned and chopped
¼ cup	pecans, chopped
1	shallot, chopped

Place the oil in the removable cooking pot and add the tenderloin. Cover the beef with the pepper and garlic salt. Set to Brown and cook and turn as the beef browns. Add the water and set to High pressure. Cook for 12 to 14 minutes. Use the quick-release method to release the pressure and remove the lid.

Place the butter in a medium saucepan and melt over medium heat. Add the blue cheese and stir until the cheese has melted. Add the broth, wine, mushrooms and pecans and heat on low heat. Add the shallot just before serving. Serve the tenderloin with the warm sauce.

New York Deli
Brisket

Serves 6 to 8

3 lbs.	beef brisket, visible fat removed
2 t.	onion powder
2 T.	garlic paste (you may substitute fresh garlic, minced)
1 T.	prepared ketchup
1 t.	Dijon mustard
1 large	yellow onion, peeled and sliced

Place the brisket on a clean surface and cover with the onion powder and garlic paste. Place in the removable cooking pot and cover the top of the brisket with the ketchup and mustard. Place the onions over the top and add enough water to cover half of the brisket. Set to High pressure and cook for 50 minutes. Use the quick-release method to release the pressure and remove the lid. If the beef is not tender and cooked through, replace the lid and pressure cook again for 10 minutes. To serve, slice the brisket against the grain.

ROSEMARY & MUSHROOM STUFFED
FLANK STEAK IN CHIANTI DEMIGLAZE

Serves 4

2 T.	extra-virgin olive oil
I small	white onion, chopped
I clove	garlic, minced
I ½ cups	Italian chianti (or choose any dry red wine)
I ½ lbs.	lean flank steak, trimmed and fat removed
I egg	lightly beaten
½ cup	crimini mushrooms, cleaned and chopped
I cup	mozzarella cheese, shredded
½ cup	soft bread crumbs
I large	egg
I t.	fresh rosemary, finely minced
I t.	salt
½ t.	black pepper, freshly ground

Place the olive oil in the removable cooking pot and set to Brown. Sauté the onion and garlic for 2 minutes until softened and add the chianti. Stir often as the wine cooks and reduces for 5 minutes. You should have at least one cup of liquid remaining. If not, add wine to equal one cup.

Place the flank steak on a clean surface. In a medium bowl, mix together the remaining ingredients. The mixture should be slightly moist and dense. Spoon the stuffing over the top of the flank steak evenly, spreading to within one inch of the edges. Beginning at one of the long sides, roll the steak with the stuffing inside. Use cooking string or ties to secure the stuffed roll.

Place the stuffed flank steak in the wine demiglaze and set to High pressure. Cook for 13 to 15 minutes. When done, use the quick-release method to release the pressure and remove the lid. Remove the string or ties and cut the steak into ½-inch thick slices to serve.

Roast Beef with Creamy
Horseradish Sauce

Serves 8

3 lbs.	beef pot roast (cross rib, chuck, etc.)
1 t.	garlic salt
½ t.	cracked black pepper
2 cups	beef broth
3 T.	butter or margarine
3 T.	flour
1½ cups	lowfat milk
3 T.	creamed horseradish
¼ cup	heavy cream
1 T.	Dijon mustard
	salt and pepper to taste

Place the beef in the removable cooking pot and cover the roast with the garlic salt and pepper. Add the beef broth. Set to High pressure and cook for 50 minutes. In a medium saucepan, melt the butter and add the flour. Mix continuously over medium-low heat until the mixture is smooth. Slowly add the milk, stirring constantly, until the sauce thickens and becomes smooth. Add the horseradish and stir again. Reduce the heat to low and add the cream and mustard. Add salt and pepper to taste and keep warm.

When the roast is done, use the quick-release method to release the pressure and remove the lid. If the beef is not tender, continue cooking under pressure for 5 to 8 minutes. Remove the roast from the pot and place on a serving platter. Serve the roast with the sauce on the side.

Stuffed Green Peppers with
Walnuts, Garlic & Tomatoes

Serves 4

1 lb.	lean ground beef
2 T.	white onion, chopped
1 clove	garlic
1 cup	dry seasoned bread crumbs
1	egg
1 t.	salt
½ t.	black pepper
¼ cup	walnuts, chopped
4 large	green bell peppers, tops removed, cored and seeded
6 oz.	can tomato paste
14.5 oz.	can diced tomatoes with juice

In a large bowl, combine the beef, onion, garlic, bread crumbs, egg, salt, pepper and walnuts. Spoon the mixture into each of the bell peppers. Place the peppers in the removable cooking pot. Mix together the tomato paste and diced tomatoes with juice and pour around the peppers. Set to High pressure and cook for 10 to12 minutes. Use the quick-release method to release the pressure and remove the lid. Serve the peppers with the remaining sauce.

ITALIAN MEATBALLS WITH
ORZO, BASIL & TOMATOES

Serves 4

1 lb.	lean ground beef
½ cup	orzo, uncooked
1 small	yellow onion, peeled and diced
1	egg, beaten
1 clove	garlic, minced
¼ cup	fresh basil, minced
1 t.	ground oregano
½ t.	black pepper
1½ t.	salt
2 cups	canned diced tomatoes with juice
½ cup	tomato juice
	Asiago cheese, grated

In a medium bowl, lightly mix together the beef, orzo, onion, egg, garlic, basil, oregano, pepper and salt. Form into 2-inch meatballs and place in the removable cooking pot. Set to Brown and turn the meatballs as they brown. Pour the diced tomatoes with juice around the meatballs. Set to High pressure. Cook for 10 minutes. Use the quick-release method to release the pressure and remove the lid. Remove the meatballs and serve with the remaining sauce and cheese as a garnish.

MIDWEST BEEF POT ROAST WITH ROOT VEGETABLES

Serves 6 to 8

2 T.	extra-virgin olive oil
3 lbs.	boneless beef roast
2 T.	flour
I t.	salt
½ t.	black pepper
½ t.	ground marjoram
½ t.	ground thyme
2 cups	beef broth
4 large	potatoes, peeled and cut into quarters
4 large	carrots, peeled and cut into 1-inch pieces
6	shallots, peeled

Place the oil in the removable cooking pot and add the roast. Set to Brown and sprinkle the flour over the roast. Turn and coat the roast with the remaining flour. Brown all sides of the roast. Sprinkle the salt, pepper, marjoram and thyme over the roast and pour the broth into the bottom of the pot. Set to High pressure. Cook for 45 minutes. Use the quick-release method to release the pressure and remove the lid. Add the potatoes, carrots and shallots to the pot. Set to High pressure and cook for 5 minutes. Release the pressure again. When done, serve the roast surrounded by the vegetables.

Slow Cooked Beef
& Beer Chili

Serves 4

1 ½ lbs.	lean ground beef
1 large	white or yellow onion, peeled and chopped
1	green bell pepper, cored and chopped
½ cup	fresh celery, chopped
2 cloves	garlic, minced
4 oz.	can diced green chilies
6 oz.	can tomato paste
4 T.	ground chili powder
1 t.	ground cumin
½ cup	dark beer
1 cup	chili sauce
1 cup	canned stewed tomatoes
½ cup	beef broth

Place the beef in the removable cooking pot and set to Brown. Cook and crumble the beef. Discard any grease. Add the remaining ingredients and stir well to mix. Set to Slow Cook and cook for 7 hours. Stir when done. Serve with condiments such as shredded cheese, onions, bacon, sour cream or salsa.

Sweet Paprika
Beef Goulash

Serves 4 to 6

2 T.	extra-virgin olive oil
3 T.	flour
1½ t.	salt
1 t.	black pepper
1½ lbs.	boneless beef chuck roast, cut into bite-sized pieces
2 T.	Hungarian sweet paprika
1	bay leaf
14.5 oz.	can whole tomatoes, with juice
2 cloves	garlic, minced
1 large	white onion, peeled and chopped
14.5 oz.	can beef broth
14.5 oz.	can corn, drained
6 oz.	wide egg noodles, cooked

Place the oil in the removable cooking pot. Set to Brown. In a self-sealing plastic bag, place the flour, salt and pepper. Add several pieces of beef to the bag and seal, tossing the flour and beef. Remove and place the beef in the cooking pot. Repeat with the remaining beef pieces. Brown the beef on all sides and add the paprika, bay leaf, whole tomatoes with juice, garlic, onion and beef broth. Set to High pressure. Cook for 20 minutes. Use the quick-release method to release the pressure and remove the lid. Remove the bay leaf, add the corn and egg noodles, and stir to mix. Serve while hot.

Hearty Beef
Stroganoff

Serves 4

1 T.	extra-virgin olive oil
1 lb.	beef sirloin, visible fat removed and cut into thin slices
½	yellow onion, diced
½ cup	beef broth
½ t.	black pepper
1 cup	fresh button mushrooms, cleaned and sliced
10.75 oz.	can 99% fat-free cream of mushroom soup, undiluted
¾ cup	lowfat sour cream
8 oz.	thin egg noodles, cooked and kept warm
	Italian flat-leaf parsley for garnish

Place the oil in the removable cooking pot and set to Brown. Add the beef slices and onion and sauté for 3 minutes. Add the beef broth and pepper. Set to High pressure and cook for 10 minutes. Use the quick-release method to release the pressure and remove the lid. Drain all but ½ cup of the broth and add the mushrooms and mushroom soup. Set to Brown and cook and stir while the soup heats. Add the sour cream and stir again to warm the sauce with the beef. To serve, place equal portions of the noodles on each plate and ladle the stroganoff over each serving. Garnish with the parsley.

CLASSIC SWISS STEAK WITH SMASHED NEW POTATOES

Serves 6 to 8

8	medium new potatoes, washed and cut into quarters
I cup	water
	salt and pepper to taste
¼ cup	butter
¼ cup	half-and-half cream
I T.	extra-virgin olive oil
3 lbs.	beef chuck steak
¼ cup	flour
2	yellow onions, peeled and sliced
28 oz.	can whole tomatoes with juice

Place the potatoes in the removable cooking pot and add the water. Bring to High pressure and cook for 5 minutes. Use the quick-release method to reduce the pressure and remove the lid. Place the drained potatoes in an ovenproof pan. Smash the potatoes with a fork or masher and add the salt and pepper to taste, butter and cream. Smash again. Keep the potatoes warm while preparing the Swiss steak.

Place the oil in the cooking pot and set to Brown. Dredge the steak in the flour and place in the oil. Brown for 3 to 4 minutes, stirring occasionally. Add the onions and tomatoes and set the pressure to High. Cook for 10 to 12 minutes. Use the quick-release method to release the pressure and remove the lid. Serve the steak with the smashed potatoes.

OLD-FASHIONED BEEF
PEPPER STEAK WITH ONIONS

Serves 4

2 T.	extra-virgin olive oil
1½ lbs.	round steak
2	white onions, peeled and thinly sliced
2 stalks	celery, sliced
2 cups	canned stewed tomatoes with juice
1½ t.	salt
1 t.	black pepper
2 large	green bell peppers, cored and sliced
¼ cup	water
2 t.	cornstarch
2 t.	soy sauce

Place the oil in the removable cooking pot and add the beef steak. Set to Brown and cook for 2 to 3 minutes. Add the onions, celery, tomatoes, salt, black pepper and green pepper strips. Set to High pressure and cook for 10 to 12 minutes.

While the steak is cooking, mix together the water, cornstarch and soy sauce. Use the quick-release method to release the pressure and remove the lid. Remove the steak and vegetables from the pot and place in a large serving bowl. Add the water and cornstarch mixture to the juices in the cooking pot. Set to Brown and cook and stir until the sauce thickens. Pour the sauce over the steak and serve at once.

SHANGHAI FIVE-SPICE
MEATY RIBS

Serves 4

1 T.	extra-virgin olive oil
3 lbs.	meaty beef ribs, cut
1 cup	water
½ t.	Chinese five-spice powder
1 t.	sugar
2 T.	dry sherry
2 T.	tamari soy sauce (substitute regular or low-sodium soy sauce)
1 clove	garlic, minced

Place the oil in the removable cooking pot and add the ribs. Set to Brown and cook and turn as the ribs brown. Mix together in a medium bowl the water, spice powder, sugar, sherry, soy sauce and garlic. Pour over the ribs. Set to High pressure and cook for 15 minutes. Use the quick-release method to release the pressure and remove the lid. Serve while warm.

20-MINUTE TENDER
BEEF RIBS

Serves 4

1 T.	extra-virgin olive oil
4 lbs.	lean beef spareribs, cut
12 oz.	bottle mild or spicy chili sauce
10 oz.	jar grape jelly

Place the oil in the removable cooking pot and set to Brown. Add the ribs and turn as they brown. In a medium bowl, blend together thoroughly the chili sauce and grape jelly. Pour the sauce over the ribs and turn the ribs to coat thoroughly. Set to High pressure and cook for 15 minutes. Use the quick-release method to release the pressure and remove the lid. Serve with the sauce, if desired.

Stadium Beef
Spareribs

Serves 4

2 T.	extra-virgin olive oil
4 lbs.	lean beef spareribs, cut
1 large	yellow onion, peeled and chopped
½ cup	ketchup
2 T.	apple cider vinegar
1 t.	Worcestershire sauce
½ t.	ground chili powder
1 T.	brown sugar
½ cup	water

Pour the oil into the removable cooking pot and set to Brown. Add half of the ribs and brown for 3 to 4 minutes. Remove and repeat with the remaining ribs. Return the ribs in the cooking pot. Scatter the onions over the ribs. Mix together the ketchup, vinegar, Worcestershire sauce, chili powder, sugar and water. Pour the sauce over the ribs, turning the ribs to coat. Set to High pressure and cook for 15 minutes. Use the quick-release method to release the pressure and remove the lid. Remove the ribs to a serving plate and serve the sauce on the side.

Chile-Rubbed Pork Loin
Chops with Rice

Serves 4

4	boneless pork loin chops, about ½-inch thick
2 T.	ground chili powder
½ t.	garlic powder
I T.	extra-virgin olive oil
I cup	long grain white rice, uncooked
I t.	salt
½ t.	black pepper
½ t.	ground chili pepper
2 T.	yellow onion, chopped
½	green bell pepper, cored and chopped
2 cups	canned stewed tomatoes with juice
¼ cup	water

Place the chops on a clean platter and rub each with the chili powder and garlic powder. Place the oil in the removable cooking pot and set to Brown. Add the chops and brown each chop, turning once. Remove the chops and add the rice to the cooking pot, browning the rice and stirring occasionally. Place the chops over the rice and add the salt, pepper, chili pepper, onion and green pepper over evenly. Pour the stewed tomatoes and water over all. Set the pressure to High and cook for 10 to 12 minutes. Use the quick-release method to release the pressure and remove the lid.

Pork Loin with Caraway & Sauerkraut

1 T.	vegetable oil
1½ lbs.	pork loin, cut into bite-sized pieces
12 oz.	dark beer
1 clove	garlic, minced
1 t.	caraway seeds
1 t.	onion powder
½ t.	salt
1 t.	dry mustard
32 oz.	jar sauerkraut with juices

Place the oil in the removable cooking pot and set to Brown. Add the pork and turn to brown on all sides. In a medium bowl, combine the beer, garlic, seeds, onion powder, salt and mustard and blend. Pour the sauerkraut over the pork chops and cover with the beer sauce. Set to High pressure and cook for 8 minutes. Use the quick-release method to release the pressure and remove the lid.

Apple Brandied
Pork Loin Chops

Serves 4

I T.	vegetable oil
4	boneless pork loin chops, about ½-inch thick
I t.	salt
½ t.	pepper
I	yellow onion, peeled and quartered
½ cup	apple brandy (substitute brandy of your choice)
½ cup	water
2 T.	butter or margarine
3 large	sweet apples, peeled, cored and sliced
2 T.	apple brandy
	pinch salt

Place the oil in the removable cooking pot and set to Brown. Add the chops and turn as the chops brown. Sprinkle each with the salt and pepper and place the onion pieces over the chops. Pour the apple brandy and water over the chops and set to High pressure. Cook for 8 to 10 minutes. Use the quick-release method to release the pressure and remove the lid. Remove the chops from the pot and keep warm. Drain the pot and wipe dry with a paper towel.

Place the butter in the cooking pot and set to Brown. Add the apple slices and coat the slices with the butter. Cook until the apples are slightly softened and add the brandy and salt. Continue cooking for 3 to 4 minutes, or until the apples are tender. To serve, cover each chop with the brandied apples and serve.

ARGENTINE PORK ROAST
WITH CHIMICHURRI SAUCE

Serves 8

1 T.	extra-virgin olive oil
2 lbs.	boneless pork roast, visible fat removed
2 cups	beef broth

Chimichurri Sauce:

¼ cup	fresh parsley, chopped
¼ cup	fresh cilantro, chopped
2 T.	extra-virgin olive oil
¼ cup	yellow onion, chopped
2 T.	fresh lemon juice
1 t.	salt
2 cloves	garlic, minced
	fresh cilantro for garnish

Place the oil in the removable cooking pot and set to Brown. Add the pork roast and turn as the roast browns. Add the beef broth. Set to High pressure and cook for 45 minutes. Use the quick-release method to release the pressure and remove the lid. Remove the roast and slice or shred.

To prepare the sauce, combine all of the remaining ingredients, except the cilantro for garnish, in a blender. Pulse until fairly smooth. Drizzle the *Chimichurri Sauce* over each slice of pork, garnish with the cilantro and serve.

CARNITAS WITH GREEN CHILE SAUCE

Serves 8

1 T.	extra-virgin olive oil
2 lbs.	pork roast, visible fat removed
1 large	yellow onion, sliced
1 T.	ground chili powder
1 T.	ground cumin
1	bay leaf
16	flour tortillas

Green Chile Sauce:

2	green tomatoes, peeled and chopped
1	tomatillo, peeled and chopped
½ cup	green onions, chopped
1 clove	garlic, minced
½ t.	salt
4 oz.	canned green chilies, chopped
1	jalapeño chile, seeded and minced
1 T.	fresh parsley, minced
1 T.	fresh cilantro, minced

Place the oil in the removable cooking pot and set to Brown. Add the roast and turn to brown on all sides. Layer the onions over the roast and sprinkle with the chili powder, cumin and bay leaf. Set to High pressure and cook for 45 minutes.

While the pork is cooking, mix together in a medium bowl all of the ingredients for the *Green Chile Sauce*. Let stand at room temperature. When the pork is done, use the quick-release method to release the pressure and remove the lid. Remove the bay leaf. Serve the pork in bowls and spoon the *Green Chile Sauce* on top of each serving.

Pork Tenderloin with
Thyme & Dijon Mustard Cream

Serves 6 to 8

2 T.	extra-virgin olive oil
2 lbs.	pork tenderloin, tied with cooking string
1 t.	salt
½ t.	coarsely ground black pepper
½ t.	onion powder
1 cup	beef broth
2 T.	flour
¼ cup	milk
1 T.	Dijon mustard
½ t.	black pepper
½ t.	salt
½ t.	dried thyme
½ cup	half-and-half cream
1 T.	fresh parsley, minced

Place the oil in the removable cooking pot and set to Brown. Add the pork tenderloin and brown, turning once or twice. Cover the pork with the salt, pepper and onion powder. Pour the broth around the tenderloin. Set to High pressure and cook for 20 to 25 minutes. Use the quick-release method to release the pressure and remove the lid. Remove the pork tenderloin and cover to keep warm.

Discard all but 1 cup of the juices in the cooking pot. Set to Brown. Whisk together the flour and milk and add to the broth. Cook and stir until the sauce is thickened and add the mustard, pepper, salt, thyme and cream. Stir to blend until the sauce is warmed throughout. To serve, slice the tenderloin and ladle the sauce over each slice. Garnish with the parsley.

Apricot-Glazed
Pork Tenderloin

Serves 6 to 8

1 T.	vegetable oil
2 lbs.	pork tenderloin, tied with cooking string
½ t.	ground sage
1 t.	black pepper
¼ cup	orange juice
1 cup	vegetable broth
2 T.	port wine
¼ cup	apricot chutney

Place the oil in the removable cooking pot and set to Brown. Add the tenderloin and brown, turning once or twice. Sprinkle the sage and pepper over the pork and pour the orange juice and vegetable broth around the meat. Set to High pressure and cook for 20 to 25 minutes. Use the quick-release method to release the pressure and remove the lid. Remove the tenderloin and slice into 1-inch thick slices. Remove the cooking juices and use a paper towel to clean the cooking pot.

Place the port wine and apricot chutney in the pot and set to Brown. Cook and stir for 2 minutes, or until the sauce is warmed throughout. Pour over the pork slices and serve.

Tequila & Lime
Pork Spareribs

Serves 5 to 6

2 T.	fresh cilantro, chopped
2 cloves	garlic, minced
2	green onions
2 t.	ground chili powder
2 jiggers	tequila
¼ cup	lime juice
¼ cup	vegetable oil
4 lbs.	pork spareribs, split

Combine the cilantro, garlic, green onions, chili powder, tequila, lime juice and oil in a large self-sealing plastic bag. Add the ribs, cover with the marinade, and seal the bag. Refrigerate for 2 to 8 hours.

Place the ribs in the removable cooking pot and add the marinade plus enough water to measure 1 cup total liquid. Set to High pressure. Cook for 25 minutes. Use the quick-release method to release the pressure and remove the lid. When done, the ribs should be cooked throughout and tender. If not, continue cooking under pressure for 5 minutes.

Savory Pork & Sausage
Cassoulet

Serves 8

1 T.	extra-virgin olive oil
1 lb.	pork loin, cut into bite-sized pieces
1 lb.	kielbasa, sliced into bite-sized pieces
½ t.	black pepper
1 T.	fresh parsley, minced
2 cloves	garlic, minced
1 small	white onion, peeled and chopped
1 cup	low-sodium chicken broth
½ cup	petite carrots, washed
15 oz.	can white cannellini beans, rinsed and drained
14.5 oz.	can diced tomatoes with juice

Combine all of the ingredients in the removable cooking pot. Set to High pressure and cook for 8 to 10 minutes. Use the quick-release method to release the pressure and remove the lid. Ladle into bowls to serve.

Jamaican Rum & Brown Sugar Ham

Serves 8 to 10

3-4 lbs.	**smoked picnic ham**
½ cup	**dark brown sugar, packed**
¼ cup	**lime juice**
½ cup	**Jamaican rum fresh pineapple slices for garnish**

Place the ham in the removable cooking pot. In a small bowl, mix together the sugar, lime juice and rum until smooth. Pour around the ham and set to High pressure. Cook for 20 to 25 minutes. Use the natural-release method to release the pressure and remove the lid. Serve the ham with the pineapple slices for garnish.

Country Ham Hocks
& Pinto Beans

Serves 4 to 6

1½ cups	dry pinto beans, sorted and cleaned
1 inch	piece salt pork (you may substitute 4 slices bacon)
2	smoked ham hocks
1 cup	yellow onion, chopped
1	green bell pepper, cored and chopped
2 cloves	garlic, minced
2 cubes	beef bouillon
2 T.	ketchup
½ t.	ground oregano
	salt and freshly ground pepper to taste
	pinch of sugar

Soak the beans overnight in a large pot of water. Drain. Place the salt pork or bacon in the removable cooking pot and set to Brown. Sauté the pork, turning occasionally, until browned on all sides. Remove and crumble or chop. Set aside.

Place the beans and ham hocks in the cooking pot and add 6 cups of water (do not exceed the maximum fill line in the cooking pot). Set to High pressure and cook for 15 minutes. When done, use the natural-release method to release the pressure and remove the lid. Remove the ham hocks and shred the meat from the bone. Return the meat to the liquid and add the onion, pepper, garlic, beef bouillon, ketchup oregano, salt, pepper, sugar and salt pork or bacon. Set to Brown and stir as the beans and sauce heat. Warm thoroughly and serve in bowls.

Pineapple Glazed
Pork Spareribs

1 T.	vegetable oil
4 lbs.	boneless pork spare ribs, cut
1 cup	pineapple preserves
¼ cup	apple cider vinegar
½ cup	ketchup
1 T.	soy sauce
2 T.	dark brown sugar
1 t.	lemon juice

Place the oil in the removable cooking pot and set to Brown. Add the spareribs and brown, turning occasionally. Add 2 cups of water and set to High pressure. Cook for 20 minutes. Use the quick-release method to release the pressure and remove the lid. Remove the ribs and discard the liquid and any visible fat on the ribs.

In the cooking pot, combine the pineapple preserves, vinegar, ketchup, soy sauce, sugar and lemon juice. Blend well and set to Brown. Add the ribs and coat each thoroughly with the pineapple glaze. Heat and stir without burning the sauce, turning the ribs as they warm throughout. Serve while hot.

LAMB WITH ARTICHOKES & LEMON

Serves 6

2 T.	extra-virgin olive oil
3 lbs.	boneless leg of lamb, cut into 2-inch pieces
1 t.	dried oregano
¼ t.	ground black pepper
1 cup	beef broth
3 T.	fresh lemon juice
4 cloves	garlic, minced
2 9 oz.	pkgs. frozen artichoke hearts, thawed
¼ cup	butter or margarine
1	lemon, sliced

Place the oil in the removable cooking pot and set to Brown. Sprinkle the lamb with the oregano and black pepper and sauté the lamb in the oil until browned on all sides. Add the broth, lemon juice, garlic and artichoke hearts. Cover and set to High pressure. Cook for 15 minutes. Release the pressure using the quick-release method and remove the lid. Gently add the butter and stir. Spoon the lamb and artichoke hearts into a serving bowl and toss with extra cooking sauce. Garnish with the lemon slices.

MEDITERRANEAN LAMB
MEDALLIONS WITH COUSCOUS

Serves 8

2 T.	extra-virgin olive oil
¼ t.	ground black pepper
1½ lbs.	boneless lamb loin
1 cup	chicken broth
½ t.	dried thyme
½ t.	ground marjoram
½ t.	ground sage
½ t.	dried mint
1	green bell pepper, cored and coarsely chopped
2 cups	instant couscous, un-cooked
	fresh chopped mint for garnish

Place the oil in the removable cooking pot and set to Brown. Press the black pepper over the lamb loin and brown all sides in the olive oil. Add the chicken broth, herbs and bell pepper. Set to High pressure and cook for 35 to 40 minutes, until the meat in the thickest part is at least 150°F for medium. Use the quick-release method to reduce the pressure and remove the lid. Remove the meat and let stand for 10 minutes.

Add water, if needed, to equal 2 cups of liquid in the cooking pot. Set to Brown and bring the liquid to a boil. Stir in the couscous. Cover and turn to Off. Let the couscous stand until the liquid has been absorbed, about 5 min. To serve, spoon the couscous into a large pasta bowl. Slice the loin into eight pieces and place on the couscous. Garnish with the mint.

Lamb & Wilted Spinach Soup

Serves 4

1 T.	extra-virgin olive oil
1	medium yellow onion, peeled and coarsely chopped
1 clove	garlic, minced
1 lb.	lamb shoulder, boneless, cut into bite-sized pieces
2 T.	Worcestershire sauce
8 oz.	can tomato sauce
3½ cups	beef broth
2 large	russet potatoes, peeled and cubed
3	carrots, peeled and sliced
1 cup	fresh baby spinach, rinsed and coarsely chopped
¼ cup	Parmesan cheese, freshly grated

Place the oil in the removable cooking pot and set to Brown. Add the onion and garlic and sauté for 1 minute. Add the meat and brown evenly. Add the Worcestershire sauce, tomato sauce, beef broth, potatoes, and carrots and set to High pressure. Cook for 8 minutes. Use the quick-release method to release the pressure and remove the lid. Add the spinach, stir and cook another minute, or just until the spinach is wilted. Serve in individual bowls topped with Parmesan cheese.

Rosemary Garlic-Studded
Lamb Roast

Serves 4

½ t.	salt
¼ t.	ground black pepper
2½ lbs.	boneless lamb roast
8 cloves	garlic, sliced
2 T.	extra-virgin olive oil
8 small	new potatoes, unpeeled
8	carrots, peeled and cut into quarters
6	medium mushrooms, halved
½ cup	dry red wine
½ cup	chicken broth
1 T.	fresh rosemary, minced

Salt and pepper the lamb roast. Cut very small slits over the surface of the roast and insert the garlic slices. Place the olive oil in the removable cooking pot and set to Brown. Place the roast in the cooking pot and sauté, turning the lamb as it browns. Place the potatoes and carrots around the roast and layer the mushrooms on top. Add the wine and chicken broth, then sprinkle with the fresh rosemary. Cover, set to High pressure, and cook for 35 to 40 minutes or until a meat thermometer registers 150°F for medium. Release the pressure using the quick-release method and remove the lid. Place the roast on a board to rest. To serve, slice the roast and surround with the vegetables. Use the cooking liquid as an au jus sauce, if desired.

Lamb Salad with Red Onion, Kalamata Olives & Feta Cheese

Serves 4 as a main course

2 T.	extra-virgin olive oil
1 lb.	boneless lamb steaks
1 cup	chicken broth
1 T.	lemon juice
1 T.	sugar
10 oz.	spring lettuce salad mix
1	medium green bell pepper, thinly sliced
1 cup	red onions, thinly sliced
6 oz.	kalamata olives, pitted and sliced
2 cups	feta cheese, crumbled
3 T.	extra-virgin olive oil
1 T.	balsamic vinegar
1 clove	garlic, minced
¼ t.	ground black pepper
2 t.	fresh dill, minced
1 t.	fresh oregano, minced

Place 2 tablespoons of olive oil in the removable cooking pot and set to Brown. Add the lamb and brown on both sides. Add the chicken broth, lemon juice and sugar. Set to High pressure and cook for 10 minutes. Release the pressure using the quick-release method and remove the lid. Remove the steaks to a cutting board and let stand for 5 minutes. Slice into ½-inch thick slices.

In a large salad bowl, toss the spring salad mix, bell pepper, onions, kalamata olives and feta cheese. In a small bowl, make the dressing by whisking together the 3 tablespoons olive oil, balsamic vinegar, garlic, black pepper, dill and oregano. Add the sliced lamb to the salad and toss all together with the dressing.

Chapter 7

DELECTABLE BREADS & DESSERTS

Chipotle Cornbread with
Roasted Red Pepper Butter

Serves 4 to 6

½ cup	butter, softened
2 T.	roasted red peppers, minced
1 cup	flour
1 cup	yellow cornmeal
3 T.	sugar
2 t.	baking powder
1 t.	salt
1 cup	buttermilk
1 cup	lowfat milk
1 large	egg, beaten
1	chipotle chile, chopped
1 T.	green chile, chopped
6 T.	butter or margarine, melted

Combine the butter and red peppers in a small decorative mold or bowl and refrigerate. In a large mixing bowl, combine the flour, cornmeal, sugar, baking powder and salt. Set aside. In a medium bowl, combine the buttermilk, lowfat milk, egg, chile and butter. Blend together and pour into the large bowl of dry ingredients. With a large spoon, mix the ingredients until just combined and no lumps remain.

Select a 1-1 ½ quart ovenproof bowl or pan that will fit into the removable cooking pot. Coat the pan liberally with shortening. Pour the bread batter into the pan. Place a steamer rack* in the cooking pot and fill with water to just below the rack. Place the pan on the rack. Cover the pan tightly with foil. Set to Steam and steam for 30 to 35 minutes, or until the center of the bread is firm. Cool on a rack for 10 minutes, cut into wedges and serve with the red pepper butter.

*You can find a steamer rack or an expandable steaming basket at many grocery and kitchen specialty stores.

TRADITIONAL BOSTON
BROWN BREAD

Serves 4 to 6

I cup	rye flour
I cup	yellow cornmeal
I cup	white flour
2 t.	baking soda
I t.	salt
¾ cup	dark molasses
2 cups	buttermilk

In a large bowl, mix together the dry ingredients. Add the molasses and buttermilk and beat until just smooth. Select a 1-1½ quart ovenproof bowl or pan that will fit into the removable cooking pot. Coat the pan liberally with shortening. Pour the bread batter into the pan.

Place a steamer rack* in the cooking pot and fill with water to just below the rack. Place the pan on the rack. Cover the pan tightly with foil. Set to Steam and steam for 35 to 45 minutes, or until the center of the bread is firm. Remove and turn the bread onto a plate.

You can find a steamer rack or an expandable steaming basket at many grocery and kitchen specialty stores.

FARMHOUSE BUTTERMILK
SPOON BREAD

Serves 6 to 8

1 cup	white cornmeal
1½ cups	boiling water
1 T.	butter or margarine
3 large	eggs, separated
1 cup	buttermilk
1 t.	salt
1 t.	sugar
1 t.	baking powder
¼ t.	baking soda

Place the cornmeal in a large bowl and add the water. Stir until no lumps remain. Cool slightly and blend in the butter and egg yolks. Beat until smooth. Add the buttermilk, salt, sugar, baking powder and soda. In a small bowl, beat the egg whites until soft peaks form and fold into the cornmeal batter. Select a 1-1½ quart ovenproof pan or bowl that will fit into the removable cooking pot. Liberally coat the pan with shortening and spoon the batter into the pan.

Place a steamer rack* in the cooking pot and fill with water to just below the rack. Place the pan on the rack. Cover the pan tightly with foil. Set to Steam and steam for 45 minutes, or until the spoonbread is slightly firm on top. Remove and spoon the bread onto individual plates.

*You can find a steamer rack or an expandable steaming basket at many grocery and kitchen specialty stores.

Golden Raisin & Walnut Bread

Serves 6 to 8

1½ cups	flour
½ cup	sugar
1 t.	baking soda
1 t.	baking powder
¼ t.	salt
1 large	egg, beaten
1 cup	apple juice
½ cup	golden raisins
½ cup	walnuts, chopped

In a large bowl, mix together the flour, sugar, soda, powder and salt. Add the egg, apple juice, raisins and walnuts and blend just until all of the ingredients are moistened. Select a 1-1½ quart ovenproof pan or bowl that will fit into the removable cooking pot. Liberally coat the pan with shortening and spoon the batter into the pan.

Place a steamer rack* in the cooking pot and fill with water to just below the rack. Place the pan on the rack. Cover the pan tightly with foil. Set to Steam and steam for 45 to 50 minutes, or until the bread is slightly firm on top. Remove and invert onto a serving plate. Cool 10 minutes before slicing.

You can find a steamer rack or an expandable steaming basket at many grocery and kitchen specialty stores.

Pumpkin Spice Bread
Pudding Laced with Cognac

Serves 4 to 6

½ cup	canned pumpkin purée
2 large	eggs, beaten
½ cup	sugar
⅔ cup	lowfat milk
¼ t.	ground nutmeg
¼ t.	ground cinnamon
1 t.	vanilla extract
pinch	salt
¼ cup	butter, melted
2 cups	day-old cinnamon bread, torn into pieces
1 T.	cognac liqueur

In a large bowl, blend the purée, eggs, sugar, milk, nutmeg, cinnamon, extract, salt and butter. Beat until smooth. Select a 1-1½ quart ovenproof pan or bowl that will fit into the removable cooking pot. Liberally coat the pan with shortening and add the bread. Pour the batter over the bread and turn the bread once over the bread to soak up the liquid as much as possible. Drizzle with the cognac and run a knife through the bread to absorb the cognac.

Place a steamer rack* in the cooking pot and fill with water to just below the rack. Place the pan on the rack. Cover the pan tightly with foil. Set to Steam and steam for 35 to 40 minutes, or until the bread is slightly firm and moist on top. Remove and cool 10 minutes before slicing.

*You can find a steamer rack or an expandable steaming basket at many grocery and kitchen specialty stores.

Sour Cream & Lemon
Cheesecake

Serves 6 to 8

½ cup	graham cracker crumbs
2 T.	butter or margarine, melted
8 oz.	pkg. cream cheese, softened
½ cup	white sugar
3 large	egg yolks
2 T.	fresh lemon juice
1 t.	pure vanilla extract
pinch	salt
1 ¼ cups	sour cream
	whipped cream for garnish

Mix the graham cracker crumbs and butter in a small bowl. Press into the bottom of a 6-inch springform pan. Using an electric mixer, blend together the cream cheese, sugar, egg yolks, lemon juice, vanilla, salt and sour cream until smooth and blended. Pour into the prepared pan. Cover the pan tightly with foil.

Place a steamer rack* in the removable cooking pot and fill with water to just below the rack. Place the pan on the rack. Set to Steam and steam for 50 to 55 minutes, or until a knife drawn through the center is clean. Remove and cool. Remove any water from the top of the foil. Refrigerate for at least 6 hours before serving. Garnish with whipped cream.

*You can find a steamer rack or an expandable steaming basket at many grocery and kitchen specialty stores.

Vanilla Bean Custard with Fresh Berry Mélange

Serves 4

1 cup	evaporated milk
1 cup	whole milk
4 large	egg yolks
⅓ cup	sugar
½ t.	pure vanilla extract
¼ t.	salt
1 whole	vanilla bean
½ cup	fresh blueberries, rinsed
½ cup	fresh blackberries, rinsed
½ cup	fresh strawberries, rinsed
2 T.	Frangelico® liqueur

In a large saucepan, heat the evaporated milk and the whole milk until hot, but not bubbling. In a medium bowl, beat the egg yolks into the sugar and add the extract and salt. Slowly add the hot milk to the egg yolk and sugar mixture, whisking constantly as they are combined. Add the vanilla bean. Return the pudding to the saucepan and heat on medium-low until the sugar is melted, about 2 to 3 minutes. Remove the vanilla bean and discard.

Coat 4 small ramekins with cooking spray and pour the custard batter evenly into each. Cover each ramekin with foil and place in the removable cooking pot. Pour enough water into the pot to reach halfway up the side of the ramekins. Set to Steam and steam for 50 to 55 minutes, or until a knife drawn through the custard comes out clean. Remove and cool. Remove any water from the top of the foil. Refrigerate for at least 6 hours before serving. To serve, combine the berries with the liqueur and spoon over each custard.

Persimmon & Date
Steamed Pudding

Serves 4

½ cup	butter or margarine
1½ cups	dark brown sugar, packed
2 large	eggs
1 t.	vanilla extract
1 cup	fresh persimmon pulp, skinned
½ t.	ground cinnamon
½ t.	salt
1 t.	baking soda
1 t.	baking powder
1 cup	flour
1 cup	dates, chopped

In a large bowl, combine the butter, sugar, eggs, vanilla, persimmon and cinnamon. Beat until smooth. Combine in a medium bowl the salt, baking soda, baking powder and flour. Add the dry ingredients to the butter/sugar mixture and beat again until smooth. Fold in the chopped dates.

Select a 1-1½ quart ovenproof pan or bowl that will fit into the removable cooking pot. Liberally coat the pan with shortening and pour the batter into the pan. Place a steamer rack* in the cooking pot and fill with water to just below the rack. Place the pan on the rack. Cover the pan tightly with foil. Set to Steam and steam for 40 to 45 minutes, or until the pudding is moist, but firm on top. Serve while warm or refrigerate up to 6 hours before serving.

You can find a steamer rack or an expandable steaming basket at many grocery and kitchen specialty stores.

BLACK & TAN
BREAD PUDDING

Serves 4

2 cups	dry white bread cubes
¼ cup	semisweet chocolate chips
¼ cup	butterscotch chips
¾ cup	whole milk
½ cup	half-and-half cream
2	eggs, beaten
1 t.	vanilla extract

Select a 1 quart ovenproof pan or bowl that will fit in the removable cooking pot and coat with cooking spray. Place the bread cubes in the pan. Cover with the chocolate and butterscotch chips. With an electric mixer, blend the milk, cream, eggs and vanilla until smooth. Pour over the bread and chips. Cover tightly with foil.

Place a steamer rack* in the cooking pot and fill with water to just below the rack. Place the pan on the rack. Set to Steam and steam for 25 to 30 minutes, or until the pudding is moist, but firm on top. Serve while warm or refrigerate up to 6 hours before serving.

*You can find a steamer rack or an expandable steaming basket at many grocery and kitchen specialty stores.

INDEX

Index

113

Index

115